THE CHOLO WHO SAID NOTHING

AND OTHER POEMS

THE CHOLO WHO SAID NOTHING

AND OTHER POEMS

by Kenneth Robert Chacón

Turning Point

Published by Turning Point

P.O. Box 541106

Cincinnati, OH 45254-1106

ISBN: 9781625492159

Poetry Editor: Kevin Walzer

Business Editor: Lori Jareo

Photography: Corina Chacón

Visit us on the web at www.turningpointbooks.com

This book is dedicated to the addicted, the lost, the broken. There is hope and it rides on clouds.

I've got to thank my familia: my sweet, patient wife Corina, my faithful, purehearted son who looks just like me, Cruz, my strong-willed, chola daughter, Marina, my handsome and incredibly funny son, Ezekiel, and my crazygoofysmart little mama, Trinity. Thank you for saving my life.

I would also like to thank my brothers and sister for all their support. Sandy, you cared for me. Rick, you carried me. Daniel, you showed me the way. To my mom and my dad, I pray I'll see you again, with perfect eyes and hearts. And to my cousin Andrew, you've been there since day one.

A special thanks to the poets and teachers I learned from: Connie Hales, Lee Herrick, Teresa Tarazi, Tim Z. Hernandez, Suzy Huerta, Michael Luis Medrano, Marisol Baca, Kevin Walzer, Lori Jareo, and so many more. Thanks for the inspiration and for helping a brother out.

I've got to give a big shout of praise to my Savior. Lord, you know I ain't perfect, but use me!

Some of these poems have appeared in the following publications:

Flies, Cockroaches, and Poets: "To the Drunk Black Man Who Gave Me Three Cigarettes"
In The Grove: "Where Will This Addiction Take Me?" and "Skinsick"
The Cimarron Review: "Varrio Gnosticism" and "The Cholo Who Said Nothing"
Poetry Quarterly: "In the Pews of Victory Life Center"
BorderSenses: "Jail Ceremony"

Contents

CROUCHING AT MY DOOR

My mother died when I was 13 and Sin has been crouching at my door ever since.

When she died, I instantly hated women.
I dreamed of them leaving me on a cold winter's night or on the eve of my birthday. I imagined the suitcase they'd use to pack their things, just when I needed them most; it was brown and worn, as brown and worn as their faces, and they carried it out the door bravely as if leaving a haunted house that had scared them one time too many. And once I pictured this image so clearly I wrote it in a short story that won a scholarship.

My mother died when I was 13 and I began to hate myself.
I stood up late nights staring into a full-length mirror while violently ironing my clothes, mouthing cusswords at my reflection, the lyrics to gangsta rap, while pressing razor sharp creases down the legs of my khakis, thin lines down the center of my shirts after snorting fat lines down the center of the mirror I'd made in shop class at De Wolf Continuation, complete with red Old English letters that read *North Side Fresno*, etched so carefully by my own hand you'd think it was God's Holy Name itself.

In those days I would leave my house early in the morning, so early the streets were dead, the only other drivers workers in shirts stitched with their first names in ovals over their hearts and I would hurl bullets, bullets like tears, into the air towards anyone who looked at me, towards anyone who looked like me, those with creases in their khakis and lines down the center of their shirts. And I'd speed off in my low-riding Honda, my heart a little lighter as if I'd accomplished something great, as if I'd squashed a million cockroaches underfoot and made the world a better place.

You see I hated myself, my station in life, but that's because Sin was crouching at my door, licking its lips with anticipation.

My mother died when I was thirteen and I cursed God.
I hated the bastard because He'd taken the one thing I'd loved most.
It was almost as if He'd searched my heart and robbed me of me what was most precious. So I stood up late nights, a glass pipe in my right hand like some newfangled prophet, shepherding the sick to get sicker, and read 3 different Bibles at a time looking for loopholes. I made lists scrawled in my best graffiti about why I should hate God, reject Jesus:

> Jesus was just a man.
> Christianity had decimated my people.
> It was the religion of the oppressor.
> It allowed for the forgiveness of people who needed
> punishing, people like me.

God had killed my mother.

And yet after graduating from college, a miracle in itself, I found
myself returning to Fresno, the same city that birthed my original Sin.
On Sunday mornings I looked to my sister, I looked to my brother,
both having been royally kicked in the ass by life, but both with purpose
on Sunday mornings, a purpose I found annoying. I would hear them
through the thin walls of the house where we all lived, the whir of their
blowdryers, the hum of their electric toothbrushes, the sounds their
Bibles would make tucked under their arms as they left for service.

Finally, they drug me with them.

And I'd stand there in the pews, the alcohol from the night before having
not yet left my breath, the meth doing jump jacks in my blood. One
afternoon a deck of cards fell from the sky and they fell in order, from
the pews to the altar, and GOOD LORD! I raised my hands in worship.

And even though Sin has been crouching at my door, waylaying
me whenever it gets the chance, God honored my desire to Find Him,
to Meet Him in the clouds, and He showed me His mercy when all I
deserved was death.

It took 4 children, 144,000 sins, and 22 pounds of meth before my mind,
my heart, was allowed to change. I never could before, but that's because
Sin was crouching at my door. And now I find myself blessed beyond

blessed, a teacher, a father, a husband, a poet, wishing to praise the Lord the best way I know how.

Dear Reader,

Welcome to it.

I. ADDICTION AND OTHER DEMONS

107 Degrees

It's 107 degrees today. What more can I say?
Fresno streets beat a steady pulse into my head,
possessing me like a demon. Downtown, wishing
I were drunk, but still I search for you in the gray
pavement haze and darker asphalt. It's this search,
this aching, that will lead me to the other side
of high where you must know I want to be.

Along Tulare, cars chase each other, mock
each other, approach each other recklessly.
Oncoming. Careening. Moving dangerously
close to the road's yellow heartbeat. I feel
the hatred that shoots from their exhausts
like curses from a lover's mouth. It's as real
as murder and the 6-inch knife I carry folded
in my pocket like an unanswered prayer.

Past Van Ness is the Fulton Mall. Many
of the buildings have also been abandoned.
They've had to watch as their doors closed
for business, store owners packing what no
one wanted, stripping walls bare in an evening

and leaving forever the next morning.
There's *joyerias* and *taquerias* and the swap
mall filled with the suits and stares of gangbangers.
This is where Koreans sell the sequined sandals
that beautiful brown mothers of beautiful brown
babies wear when they dance or when they walk
the slanted streets towards bus stops, county
offices, or the jail's concrete visiting rooms,
pushing strollers along as if they were trophies.

I look for you inside the 3 for $10 T-shirts
of Fulton, their heavy designs of black and silver,
of lowriders and *cholos*, of long haired women
and clowns who weep, of guns and sad eyed
jesuses who bleed from the head. Before long, I
forget what I've been looking for. Am I looking
for God's hiding place within the heat and concrete?
Or am I looking for the mother of my children
who touches me softly on those nights when I can see,
so clearly, that the world is shit, the same woman
who slipped through my fingers last night when I
watched my hand shrink into a fist? Or am I looking
for the simple pleasure of a rock to fill my pipe
to begin my easy descent into an early heaven?
I don't know the answer. All I know is the weight

of the sun, the push it makes against my neck.

It's 107 degrees and the streets look drunk today
and every 20 minutes some *puto* tries to punk me
and whenever I look up there's a cop staring,
and I can't help but think of my son, my daughter,
expect to see them in an alley, the bottoms of their
feet caked with mud, their hair matted, their faces
clean only where their tears have trailed.

Damn this sobriety. Each time I'm sober the city sings
to me of a new city that sleeps, under all the heat,
under all the cement that's been freely poured the way
I've heard God's spirit is poured on Sunday mornings.
I start to sob because I know it must be peeled away,
this stubborn city, to reveal what is truly important.

But it's 107 degrees and I've forgotten what I'm looking
for. The streets are drunk, swaying back and forth
like liquor. Passing by a corner store, I smell whiskey
and dust and 3 bums sitting in front yelling, *I love you!*
to any woman. I sit down beside them and enjoy the graffiti.

WHERE WILL THIS ADDICTION TAKE ME?

Tonight it takes me to a liquor store parking lot,
corner of Fruit and Olive. Minutes ago, it took
me, my car, its worn-down tires, into a ripe
nail, starving for attention. And in this night
that refuses to play nice, to fold softly away
and breed daylight, I sit on the pockmarked
concrete, waiting for the dopeman's good
shit.

I sit waiting for the good shit and a 1/2 empty
can of Fix-A-Flat he said he might have, praying
it'll be enough to patch. And in between breaths,
beseeches to the Lord God who resides resolutely
in the sky, I think of my family waiting faithfully
at home. I think of my wife's smile, my son's
ears, my daughter's hair that smells of
fruit.

I should be above all this, above glass pipes
that shatter, above 20 rocks that are never enough,
above the dark harvests of stale things grown strong
in moonlight, shadows spreading like dandelion,

the darkness blossoming into street corners

and liquor stores where men cradle porn.

But the time is not right, water not yet wine,

and I sit waiting for the dopeman's good

shit.

OH DEAR

I imagine when you first find me
like this, sprawled across our living
room floor, your big, brown eyes
will tear, but then, when you see
the glass pipe gleaming defiantly
in my cold, sweaty palm, your dark
eyes will tear with something else.

You'll be pissed.

And it's this terrific fear
of you, my dear, the fear of the harsh
words you'll hurl at me forever, the fear
of seeing your face with that severe
expression that shows the exact weight
and measurement of my sins,
of how thoroughly I've disappointed you,
yet again, that almost makes me want
to come back. But your anger is a shadow.
Even now it fades like smoke,
like the weak flame of an empty lighter.

Even if I could resurrect,

I'd probably take another hit.

THIS GUN

There's a gun behind everything.

    There's a gun behind the stare of the man in front of you

        as you stand in line at the corner liquor store,

            a cold bottle sweating in your shaky hand.

    His stare tells you just how big his gun is,

        his pupils, large and dark, approximate the size

            of the hole the slug will leave in your ear.

There's a gun behind everything.

    There's a gun, cocked and ready, behind the tinted windows

        of the Dodge that passes you in the parking lot as

            your kids sit in the backseat strapped to car seats,

                singing songs with meaningless lyrics

                    that are never the same the second

                      time.

There's a gun behind the glassy eyes of the students as they sit

    in the classroom, scratching at their heads with itchy trigger

        fingers, staring at the place where the substitute's heart

        beats violently.

    Inside, these students are animals, beating their chests with fists,

        throwing feces at the walls, at each other, at the sub,

            a heavy, young woman whose polite words fall

like hairs from a brush when she tries to

show them math or the awkward

pause of a comma.

There's a gun behind everything.

There's a gun behind the disquieted whir

of the ghetto bird that scythes the skyline

of this *varrio*

Sometimes I feel God's hot stare on my neck

as He looks down at me through the scope

of a loaded rifle.

There's a gun behind everything.

If you look close enough, you can see the gun behind

each one of these words.

I'm holding it,

gripping the handle,

thinking of squeezing,

unsure of what to think of

people who look to poetry for answers.

To The Drunk Black Man Who Gave Me 3 Cigarettes

I was looking out for the train when I
spotted you, a slender, dark man stumbling
near the tracks, a stain on the horizon.
I was sitting on a concrete bench,
irate with heat, when I noticed
your blue plaid shirt and blue cap upturned.
Crip, I thought and maybe you were.

It was summer, late summer, on one of those
evenings when the sun feels evil and you can
do nothing but accuse it of instigating
violence like an unshaven father pushing
his son towards a fight, demanding first blood.
These are the evenings that end in regret.

I pulled the red rag from my back pocket
and flung it over my shoulder as if I'd won
it in some manly sport. I watched you walk
toward the station and my knuckles curled
into fists. I imagine them now 2 angry bulbs,
aching to bloom, but you didn't notice them.

Instead you spit a loogey like only a smoker

could and approached a man who looked anxious

and told him a story about you, a cop, and a crack

pipe; I watched you act out the arrest, telling

the man, *You know that pipe wasn't mine,*

man. You know me, man!

Of course, the man didn't know and would never know.

Or maybe I've got it wrong. Maybe he thought

of you years later as I do now and has already written

a poem, offering it like an olive branch, hoping it'll soothe

like a lozenge. Who can know? But it wasn't long until

you caught me eyeing you. You walked towards me,

saw the tattoo across my forearm, scoffed. What did you see?

Did you see me running? Did you know about my problems

with dope, cops, and the color blue? What was it?

Back then, I thought myself formidable with no fear,

but when you sat on the bench next to me,

breath like peppermint, I wanted you gone.

I'll never forget how you looked into my eyes,

your own ready to roll back into your head, and said,

I know you, man. You're a gangsta gonna turn God.

You reached into your pocket and pulled out a crushed

box of Marlboro reds. You forced 3 cigarettes

into my hand and said, *Take 'em and when you get*
to heaven, my man, tell Him a poor, black man gave
you his only treasure. Tell Him a poor man did.

I pushed the cigarettes back into your hand,
told you I didn't smoke. You shoved them back.
Just take 'em. Smoke 'em. Sell 'em. Do whatever.
It's a gift. And it wasn't until long after I hit you,
long after your nose ran red and my knuckle bruised
blue, long after I boarded the train and watched
you from my seat, fighting back tears, that I finally
take this chance to apologize.

FIX

"I saw the best minds of my generation destroyed by madness, starving
hysterical naked,
dragging themselves through the negro streets at dawn looking for an angry
fix . . ."—Allen Ginsberg, "Howl"

it all comes down to this:

      the fact that i've spent 1/2 my life on drugs and the other 1/2

            thinking about them or trying to buy them

    and i really don't care or so i would tell myself

circles of blue smoke circumnavigate my face

    my scalp my lungs my body the cankerous cracks

      of this ceiling my damp room and all this shitty furniture

and it's the lines the breaks

    the cracks the cranks that do it for me

      America loves its cracks and cranks

    and i'm no different

to tell you the truth i spent onehundredtwentyseven hours

    downloading pornography last month

      what of it

and yes i do have a catholicchristian conscience

    thanks for asking

      America loves its porn and i'm no different

even now as i write this

    as i sit here and type

i'm drowned in clouds

and distracted by a browser filled with an

endless assortment of namelessnakednouns

America loves its guns

don't think i won't shoot

i just saw my neighbor's kid at the corner store

he said *hi! do you have any bullets?* i said *why?*

he said *problems in high school! problems in high school!*

America loves its problems in high school

quit hogging the pipe America

pass that shit

i need to smoke my way to blue heaven before six

church starts at six

i'm sick i need my fix

hurry up before Jesus comes   He'll be upset

bring me the bubble America,

so i can toss in the rocks

i'll use your lighter for now

but thanks to one of your predatory lenders

i'll be able to buy my own one day

but gas prices are so high

i'm afraid they're getting higher

sometimes i have wet dreams of premium

sometimes i suffer from SUV-envy

i need gas

i need energy

i need to gogogo

like i went the night i left my wife

the night i left my daughter was stinking

and in need of a diaper change

in need of any change

later that night i ran to my pipe and changed my tune

with my pipe

i led all the cracks out of the

hardcoreexplicitraging streets

of America into Germany

later i smoked Germany

i'm a patriot if you ask my mother

America loves changing tunes

and i'm rambling again but God's grace is grafted in my noggin'

it's so sincere so near

in fact i just traded it for a dime sack

and i'm about to smoke it

but Jesus isn't angry

Jesus is never angry

He just keeps pacingpacingpacing somewhere

above the blue clouds

i can't be sure though

it's smoky in here

i can't see Him

but I know He's there

He's pacing and He's frowning and He's showing me

the wounds of His hands

and He's telling me how much He's suffered

and I know he's suffered and i'm sorry

had America and i been around at the time of the crucifixion

we could've fixed things

we could've made things right

i would've ridden on the back of a blackhawkhelicopter

parachuted down the spine of golgotha's hill

torn out the nails with my teeth

but America and i have arrived too late

all its capital and all my incoherent prayers lead us nowhere

thank God

America

that blue smoke is a sure cure for

suffering

Jesus On The Mainline

You were talking in your sleep again last
night, she says. And I say, *Bullshit.* You were,
she says. *And what was I saying?* I ask,
feeling my eyes roll at her words so damned
dismissively. *You were talking to God,*
she says matter-of-factly as if it weren't un-
common to have Jesus on the main line

      Tell Him what you want.

You were saying you were sorry, she says.
At first I thought you were saying sorry
to me and I was waiting for it, a confession.
I sat up in bed to brace myself for it,
but your eyes were closed. You were talking
to God, telling Him you would change,
that you wanted to change, but you needed help.

Oh yeah, I say. I reach for the remote, press up
until I hit the Spanish channel. *This is serious,*
she says. *At first I thought you were tripping,*
you know, because you haven't slept in a few days,
at least I haven't seen you, but you kept saying it,

you were going to change over and over. She sits up.
Looks me in the eyes. *You started crying,* she says,
and then you were on the floor, on your knees,
your hands lifted up. She looks at me, waits for me
to say something, her brown eyes shining into tears.

On the TV there's a line of dark women dancing
in sequin. They shake their tatas like they're plugged
in. *Bullshit,* I say, wanting so badly for words to be Truth.

BACKSLIDER

Underneath it all, Hell swallows.
From the sanctuary of one of the city's
churches, I hear it bellowing, casting
aspersions, gurgling perversions
like the warm muck that bubbles
out of holes in the earth. I can't listen
to worship songs without picturing
something sinful, something carnal.
I get on my knees. I get on my knees.

This Hell mocks me whenever I raise
my hands and worship the Holy One,
the Ancient of Days, on the few occasions
when I'm determined to know nothing
but Christ and Him crucified.

And when I find myself, so often now,
mounting the lusty streets at midnight, glass
pipe in hand, determined to blow everything
I have in favor of that which is cursory,
fleeting, like a kingdom of smoke,
I hear the charges brought against me:

motherless man

  father of four

    lover of one

      disciple of harsh smoke and strange women

       obsessed with corner stores

Victory is mine! I shout to drown out the voice

of my accuser, but inevitably I find myself

in a cracked alley somewhere, a polluted

heaven, listening to the hissing from underneath

concrete calling me infidel of the city.

SLAVE TO SIN

As God looks down at me

    through His holy TV screen in the sky

        I realize I'm a moving picture, streaming video,

        a sad, predictable puppet show,

        He knows, a slave to sin, which begs the question:

            Will He change the channel?

O Lord, Lord, certainly You know me.

    Lord, Lord, please don't forget me.

        I'm Your servant despite the vast cisterns of sin

        swelling up inside me.

            Will You change the channel?

            Why must everything be so black or white?

I'm unspiritual. That's my biggest problem,

    always has been.

        Plus this damned attention deficit disorder thing.

        I can't keep my mind in line for a second.

        Forgive me. Forgive me.

            How many times will You forgive me?

Lord, Lord, open up the gates of heaven, of glory,

    of middle class suburbia constructed over 144,000 American

    Indian graves.

        No. That's not right.

Delete that last part.

It sounds too much like righteous, indigenous

indignation. Move to a smooth transition.

Lord, Lord, You've known me since I was that chubby, pig-

fleshed ball of goo, unhappy squatter, in my mother's womb.

Truthfully, I'm a slave to sin and there's not much hope

for liberation,

no underground railroad to sneak me up north,

seems I'm predestined for a southbound ride.

But will You change the channel?

My only redeeming quality is that whenever I think of Your Christ

I want to whistle, shepherd the weak, be a super hero,

bring whole villages half a world away to the door of

Grace and Mercy,

have them knock,

Come on in. We've been expecting you.

I want to rouse repentance with Truth from my eyes, the ministry

of my voice, the righteous grasp of my calloused hands.

But right now I'm a slave to sin, and I'm afraid

You'll change the channel.

I'm not black or white.

What does that have to do with Christ?

Nothing.

Nothing.

I tell you nothing. I'll fix it on the edit.

I'm just a short Chicano who wishes to sing sweet worship songs

      to the Great Savior in the sky using words like

            Kentucky and Tacoma

            Byzantium and Aztlán

            Fresno and California

            Chicano and Christian,   but

currently the only lyrics that fall from my mouth

            concern words like boob or body,

            choruses that glorify everything that's sinful and bawdy.

                    Lord, how many times will You forgive me?

I'm just a short Chicano, raised barely Catholic,

      I never knew I'd grow up to be non-denominational

            unPentecostal

            irredeemable

            irretrievable

            etcetera etcetera.

I'm a slave to sin, etcetera, etcetera, but I'm not white.

      I'm the lukewarm bluegrey hue of my bouncing *Star Wars*

            screensaver.

            My screensaver turns on every two minutes.

            So do I.

            I'm a slave to sin.

                    Will You change the channel?

And I'm not black.

      I'm the tattooed *vato* on the back of the bus yelling

What are you looking at, punk?

but meaning

Repent and be baptized!

I'm the school boy Hispanic sitting in a million Taco Bell drive thrus

across the Southwest spending what's left of my financial aid

check, ordering long and often, refusing to use the

accents of my ancestors.

Not-Chose. Boar-Eat-Toes. Case-A-Deus.

Biggie size.

Biggie size.

Everything must be biggie sized.

As You can plainly see I'm a slave to sin.

Will You change the channel?

I'm just a short Chicano who wants to be the short Chicano

you can find at your local liquor store,

pacing through the aisles

furiously quoting Acts 2:39.

I could keep going on like this, Lord,

but I know You already know.

You see me when I'm searching for something good on cable

and I'm tempted by the voluptuous women in the desert

of the Spanish stations,

my TV on mute lest I learn the language.

And you see me when I read my NIV, when I fast and pray for 3 straight

days, taking only water and coffee and occasionally cocaine.

You see me, you always see me, and I'm sure it's obvious by now:

I *so* need a tan. I'm *so* pale.

I think I'll sit in the sun a while.

I'll sit outside or maybe I'll go inside and cool off.

I'm not sure. It's a scorcher outside.

Where are you going with this?

I'm not sure.

Bring back Christ somehow.

Bring him back!

I'll follow Christ, that's what'll do.

I'll run from the sun. I'll run to the son.

I'll be judged according to my faith. I'll get skin cancer.

I'll never be white unless I stay inside this summer.

Then I can turn the pasty, chalky color of my colorless room.

I'll watch women like a phantom from the balcony

of my colorless room.

I'll plant my chin on my hands and my elbows on the window sill.

Will you click on the X of my window?

Will You change the channel?

When I was a kid, I pictured Heaven the way a Chicano Studies professor

describes Aztlán:

144,000 brown skinned men, women, and angels

nestled in God's golden living room,

watching all brown sitcoms on illegal cable.

speaking Spanish and *caló* and Nahuatl at will.

And excuse me, Señor, but I'd like to ask:

> *Why can't it be?*

Needless to say, I'm a midgrade beige,

> a coconut maybe, but not quite white.

> *God change this channel!*

Lord, Lord You know it's true:

> When I was young, I loved the TV so much I hated to turn it off.
>> I'd feel so lost.
>> The voices and faces and noises from the tube were my
>> friends and I never wanted to say goodbye, never wanted

to pray.

> I would stay up to the early hours of the morning

watching whatever,

>> *Different Strokes*, Charles Bronson, *The Stepford Wives*,
>> a Catholic soundtrack of Hail Marys
>> played to the backdrop of some holy spot,
>> an altar, a rock, a tomb,
>> everything looking as certain as black
>> and as certain as white.

And there I was

> a confused brown boy suffering
>> from a lack of faith
>> from ADHD
>> from the loss of culture and language
>> from albinoism.

41

And I would flip in and out of beautiful lives without care or concern,

leaving one behind just as soon as another.

Now what kind of life is that?

SKINSICK

It just so happens that I'm sick of this world, sick
of the rotting flesh that overwhelms me like mud
on a pearl. If I were to shed my skin, if I were to peel
this flesh like a layer of clothing, you would see there
is something beautiful. I have to believe this. I chant
it aloud from dark street corners when low-hanging
branches of shadow brush over me. I repeat it like a prayer,
pleading for my life, the lives of my children in a feeble
attempt to appease an angry god. It's the only thing
that comforts me as I count down the minutes until night
hits, watching my children from a cracked window
as they play in gutters and dirt and the sparse grass
in between these shit apartments.

         And when I call my children home
before the darkness grows, before it spreads like wild
vines, I ask myself, *What else is there?* This empty glass
pipe? This loaded gun? The streets luring me away
like an adulterous woman? Or is it the moon hanging
in the night like fruit, ripening in the darkness,

                begging to be plucked?

Violin and Piano

—Listening to Max Richter's "Mercy" and reading the paper

Woe sits on my finger-
tips. I drag my hand
across the table and raise
it to my mouth. Taste.

Dumpster babies addicted.
Bitter are the shrieks
of a child's scream,
syllables of a language
we've all unlearned,

How can you do this,
mother? How can you look
into my eyes, your eyes,
and leave me here?

This is not the meal
I asked for. The ink
from the newspapers
stains my palms, black
death, sadness festering

inside of everything.

Towards the back
of the Bee, I read about the father
who pulled his child
into his arms, the height of the world
for someone so young,
and he released her, the violin quavering   alone.
She flew off a bridge
into Heaven, the strings
plucked.

The chords of the piano
are dissonant. I wait
for their soft return,
for the strokes of a key
to rise like children's
laughter before the squeals
began, before these
stories scored them-
selves into me, the violins
disturbing my peace.

At night, these words
I read nibble at my ribs,

gnawing like a child
on a breast, teeth push-
ing through. I wonder
what they taste? This
man who sees Christ,
a promise, this man
who waits for the piano's
soft return.

In the morning, woe
will sit on my fingertips
and I will eat again,
the tempo adagio,
stirring in the pit of my stomach.

II.   GRACE AND OTHER MERCIES

MY TATTOOS STILL SPEAK

My tattoos still speak even when I don't.

    North Side Fresno Bulldogs they say and confront
people I've never met and some I have and wish

    I hadn't. They speak of times in my life I'm not really
sure happened until I step from a shower and see

    them in a foggy mirror. They're imprinted on my mind,
my body, and everyone can see them. I wear them and they wear me.

My tattoos still speak even when I can't.

    It's been so long since I've plucked an angry gun
off an evil vine, pointed it, my hand not quite

    trembling, and felt the easy squeeze of a trigger.
I can't remember the way my hand looks wearing

    a glass pipe or the exact weight of an eight ball.
But once I greeted every man with a nod of the head

    laden with a heavy, hate-filled stare. I decorated
my coffee and end tables with red bandanas, everywhere red

    bandanas, and blared gangsta rap until my ears bled.

This isn't a confessional.

    My tattoos won't shut up long enough for it to be.

But now I read Rilke & Ginsberg, Lorca & Yeats,

      Wright & Neruda. Meanwhile my friends,

my only true friends, bleed into the streets

      of McKinley & West, Kings & Chestnut, Dakota & Pleasant,

their bodies battered by cops, by bullets, by each other,

      by the incessant hum of a tattoo gun.

How can I ever deny them, flesh of my flesh?

      But what to do? Have them removed? Should I lead

the quiet life of a graduate, letting people point to me as proof

      you can "get out," whipping out my degree

whenever my tattoos speak too loudly? Should I dance

      around the English departments of central California's

community colleges, become a full-time adjunct instructor

      dressed in tweed and Target,

reciting my favorite lines from "Twelfth Night?"

      Wouldn't that be erasing my life's truest poem?

To Scott Randall Faurie: July 31, 1975-March 14, 1997

Yes, Scott, I remember you.
I remember you wore the same nylon pants,
you called them slicks, day in and day out,
only bothering to change T shirts, socks, and boxers,
occasionally.

Yes, Scott, I remember you.
The first time I met you, we picked you up
at your mom's house, only a block away
from where I'd lived all my life. I'd been keeping clean,
enrolled in school, something you always said you
should do. I hadn't kicked it with the homies for a while.
Riding in the back of Rod Dog's '78 Monte Carlo
I tried to listen to what they said about you
in between injections from 12 inch subwoofers.
The word was you were a straight white boy
who happened to live in the *varrio* and you liked to walk
down the streets with huge headphones, bobbing your head,
smoking a harmless joint.

Yes, Scott, I remember you.

I remember you gave me my first porno flick.
I was shocked by the carefree way you plucked it
from your kitchen cabinet off a stack at least 10 bibles
high like a doctor prescribing medication to cure
what ailed me. You told me, *Take it home. Bring it back
when you're done.* And although I acted disgusted,
I did exactly what you said.

Yes, Scott, I remember it wasn't long after that
when we began to box ourselves into dark rooms,
sucking back on the glass dick, a welder's torch the only light
between us. I remember carefully passing the pipe
as if it were made of diamonds until the sun fought
its way through thick drapes, accusing like a police spotlight.

And yes, Scott, I know that you died before your son
Joseph was born in a year when death was everywhere
and a measly 100 bucks was more than a fair price for a life.
That year the heat haunted the city even through the night
and citizens became drunk with moonlight and young bodies
like yours often pooled on warm concrete until morning.

You see, Scott, I remember that look you gave the night
I threatened to fight you over a PlayStation. I cried
when you said, *I don't want to fight you over a stupid game,*

and I looked into those big, innocent, Arabian eyes,

and I was sorry. I'm still sorry, Scott. I've learned so much

although it took these 7 years to sink in. I know

that the homies' love was true, as true as a bullet wound,

but they showed it best by selling us fat 20 sacks and 1/16ths

for a gram's price. And it's these gems of sickness

I've been reflecting on since you left. Their luster darkens

the eye although it takes time, sometimes an entire life, to see it.

And it forces me to write this.

FICKLE SKY

Sit with me in my car as I drive
through a parking lot looking
for a spot to stop 10 feet closer
than the last one. Or as I roll through
a drive-thru 2 feet at a time, cussing
from the back of the line, when the sky
catches me by surprise and the dingy lid
of this city seems ready to peel away
and expose the insolence of this modern life.

The sky could open up.

It's in mind numbing moments
like these that I realize one day
the sky will split wide and reveal
glory, a glory to be seen and heard
and smelled between shots of exhaust,
the outrageous musk of gasoline,
the cruel, meticulous science of red lights,
the commonplace vanity of our every day.

And the sky could open up.

Isn't it funny that the sky is clearest

when I'm in my car, an inch of metal

encasing me like a pomegranate seed?

Yet on days like these, I'm amazed.

This sky. This city. So many people.

Enough not to care about. And most days

I don't care. Most days I scamper across

the floor of the sky down the freeway at 5,

weaving in and out of 2 or 3, flipping off 4,

and speeding past another 5, my tunes

turned up until my ears bleed. Most

days I can think *fuck them, fuck them all,*

and mean it and move on, home

in time for whatever's on TV.

But some days I get caught up, caged

between red lights, where a strange

feeling forces me to search the faces

of the endless at bus stops and intersections

along the avenues. Some days these faces

are too familiar and I feel like I know them,

each one, and their names could burst from

my tongue as if someone were squeezing

them from me like juice from a grape.

Then it dawns on me: these people
are alive, they're women and men,
sons and daughters, living under
the incredible weight of the sky.
And they're also waiting.

                          One day, the sky will open up.

But today, it doesn't.

VARRIO GNOSTICISM

This morning I rise to a chorus of gunfire,
each bullet's song shatters the silence
of the young morning, the gap that fills
the space between sweltering days.

I listen closely.

The tune dies. I wait for it to pick
up again, for gunshots to ring like thunder
as if an orchestra of fallen angels
were playing, trying to rip peace in half
as if it were a paper bag from the liquor store.

I listen,
        but outside,
                nothing.

I close my eyes and breathe deeply, imagining
hot lead scorching the sky before returning
to this world in its margins, this lonely *varrio*,
its descent quicker than lightning's strike.

I wonder what hand pulled the trigger,

what circumstances provoked it,

what rationale could be made.

      Was there a woman involved?

              jealousy

                    deceit

        fear

                              conceit

or merely desire biting at the body,

forcing one to risk everything

for the empty promises flesh makes.

What justification can be made?

On weekdays like this, my children

have left for the school where they play

dodgeball, eat red gelatin squares, shoot

other children with terrible cooties,

and, whenever fire drills or practice

evacuations allow, try to learn.

I wonder if my daughter heard the shots

while standing in front of the preschool

bungalow ready for recess and monkey

bars. I wonder if she noticed how the bullets'

blare seemed to hang in the air, out of tune,
unashamed, like a drunken man challenging
anyone who will listen. I wonder if she now
glares at the sky, distrustfully, protecting
herself with her thin arms, dark from sun,
half expecting something mean to fall down.

I wonder if my son heard the gun while playing
on the jungle gym, dangling upside down
from the bends of his knees, suspended
above the sandbox, concerned. I wonder
if his wide grin has returned. I wait for the phone
to ring, expect to find the tenor of a nurse's voice
on the other side. But when I pick up the phone,
         on the other side,
                  nothing.

For so long I've wanted to believe the *varrio*
a beautiful but fickle flower capable of blossoming
at any hour. I've ignored the signs scrawled
all over the walls of my apartment complex,
choosing instead to pretend the sky permanent
and mute. But the *varrio* is no flower.

We've lied to ourselves since the beginning

even after Enoch tore the scales

from our eyes, showed us how the sky dog-

ears at its very edges like the yellowed pages

of an old book, a hymnal with songs

the congregation no longer sings.

If we would only tug at the corner,

pull the page across the horizon,

we could see:

           The sky is nothing.

              The moon broken.

                 The sun asleep.

          See how the stars are thrown down?

To My Son In The Summer Of 2001

In the heat of late August, we watch
video of Christmas '98 and I make playful remarks
about how cute you *used* to be and about how
many *mocos* you had in your small but productive
5-year-old nose.

'98 was the year the heavens
gave us snow like a gift we had no idea what
to do with. I want to tell you, *mijo*, not all places
are the blacktop and rough sun and metal reflecting
like mirror you've known your entire life.

In some places, snow falls on streets
and cars so often no even one cares. But in '98 we heard
wind thundering against church windows and we walked
outside and watched snow float down into our hair
and into open trashcans and we lifted it from the ground
and held on until our tanned hands went numb.

I know you remember the ice we hurled,
but do you remember anything else? '98 was the year
I left, the year I boarded a bus and didn't come back
until Christmas, the year it snowed in Fresno.

So now, in the heat of August,

after I pull the tape from a box, I sit anxiously

and watch and think of the cold of that year.

In The Pews Of Victory Life Center

I had never kissed my son before.
I know it sounds strange to say,
but I had never kissed him in his 14
years of life. Not once had I stooped
my head and put my lips to him,
to taste him, the oils of his skin,
to breathe him in, flesh of my flesh.

I have always loved him, my son,
this gentle, wide-eyed young man
who grew up looking at me distrustfully
on those nights when I came to steal
his mother, to lock her up in a room
for about an hour, until I was done.

For this, I'd been left with regret.
It weighed on my neck, prevented
me from looking him in the eye
when we crossed paths in the hallway.
It forced a stern tone into my mouth
when I spoke to him, my voice
sounding like holes being kicked

into walls, like toys trampled underfoot.

But one day, I watched my son
as we sat in morning service, noticed
how he kept looking at himself, fiddling
with his shoes, straightening his shirt,
patting his hair, and I felt the music's
grace and kissed him. Just before I
pressed my lips against his forehead
softly the way I imagine Jesus will kiss
me one day, I drew him close, wrapped
my arms around the sinewy muscles
of his back as he leaned in uncertainly,
hesitating as if it were a trap, and I took it in,
the heaviness of his heart, which is mine.

TO MY SON AND MY DAUGHTER

"He is waiting at the edge of the sky,

and we are saved."—Andres Montoya, "hope"

Because nothing good has ever come from my life but you two

    and your very names are prayers

        that have been answered,

because in this world of shit and filth and fuck and mud of the grave

    I want to rise to raise you above my head

        where Christ rides clouds like sea,

because in this world where there is weeping, where there is gnashing

    of teeth, where even your father is wrong,

        I pray the Holy Spirit stoops to kiss your heads

            before that brutal night falls,

because like moths our lives mean nothing, fleeing with a finger's touch,

    and because I can hear, in the hollows of my ears,

        the echo of an empty tomb,

that is why I ask you, son, daughter, to reach for the Christ in the sky,

    so that you will be lifted

        to the right hand of the Father.

Please see, I tried holding onto your mother, but I faltered in sin,

    so now I have nothing but you two and the promise

        of a Murdered Man.

TO EZEKIEL ROBERT CHACÓN

Listen to me.
You see, I'm weak, I'm dying,
or maybe I'm already dead.
Whatever the case,
there is nothing more important
than what I'm about to tell you, *mijo*.

We die,
every day we die,
and that's your earthly inheritance.

We die on wedding nights
spent in pink hotel rooms,
lying next to a stranger
who says they will love us forever,
our skin smelling like gentle
bubbles and twenty dollar bills.
We die while worrying,
while warring,
while praying for peace to return
like a Christmas ornament
we had forgotten about.

We die with catheters
pinned to us like carnations.
We die with haircuts
we never should have paid for
and with yesterday's underwear
clinging to us like chewing gum.
We die in beds and in living rooms
and in 7 car pileups, our bodies spilt
over the road like salt over meat.

When I was a child,
I watched my mother,
your grandmother,
a woman you've never met,
pour small piles
of salt into her palm
and then lick it up as if she were a young,
eager lamb being fed by the hand
of a child in a petting zoo.
Months later,
I watched that same woman disappear
into her eyelids and into her cheekbones,
while her stomach turned
into a pair of harps,
her ribs springing from her

as if they would become wings.
She was dying, my own mother,
cancer nipping at her heels the way I had done
12 years before
as a hot-tempered child,
much like you are now, as I write this,
the way I'll always remember you,
fighting at your mother's breast,
your face as crimson as a gunshot wound.
I know this is tiresome,
but I may not get another chance.

Let Christ take control.
Let Him enter you.
Let Him fill you up
like salt into a shaker.
Open your mind to Him
like when you first opened your eyes
to see your mother.
Open your heart to Him like you open
your mouth to take the *chupón*.
Open your Spirit
just as you open your arms each morning
to be lifted from your crib.

I know you can't possibly remember this,

the instant way you grow so sad,

your face so darkened,

when you see your mother disappear

underneath bed covers,

only to reappear to you,

your nervous laughter, your smile.

I know you won't remember,

but I do,

and this is what I leave you.

TAKE

I carry everything in front of me seated in the curves
of my hands. My fears weigh the most; they bind
my neck at night, so they're the first to go. I carry my loves,
but it's impossible to tell where they end and where the fears
begin. And though the very thought bites at my chest,
though it hurts like the first time I had the wind knocked out
of me in my mother's front yard, these too must go.
I've stopped trying to figure things out, so here are my philosophies,
my axioms, the ghetto proverbs that I've passed as wisdom.
And even though they are few, sporadic like the hair that grows
on my toes, here are my successes. Perhaps they have done the most
damage.

All this is much too heavy. I'm afraid I'll drop them, be forced
to watch them shatter like the mirror I made at De Wolf Continuation,
the mirror that read my name in red letters next to white hands clasped
in prayer, the words *North Side Fresno* along the bottom.
I knew one day I'd break that mirror. And it did break the night
I was driven mad by meth, every shadow a broken dream, every
sound malevolent laughter, each shard a piece of my life that I'd made
shit.

Before that happens, Lord,

I'm asking You to take these things,

do what You will with them, but replace this heaviness with

something else,

something better,

something bright,

that remains.

HIGH AGAIN, I MAKE A PROMISE TO MY WIFE

-to Corina

It's been 20 years
since our bodies started banging together dumbly
puddling into one obtuse object
One in the eyes of God

But we've only been one
for 12 according to the text box
of tax bracket stamped with the golden seal
of California
the State that fought to split
us apart as teens
pulling at your heel with the promise
of food stamps and Section 8
meals and warmth
those things I could not provide

But the Lord is One.

Here we are many years later
our story defiant as it winds
through the hallway of two decades
the laughter of children filling the spaces

as familiar as the faux goose feather

comforter that covers us now

Your strong

padded frame has always been there

when I've reached for it

my lamb's heart clambering against

the cage of my body

the bedposts about to sing

the cast iron about to play out its symphony

timbre climbing walls until everyone must hear

I have no more secrets

no more apologies

no smart answers to deflect

I have always been a tether

a burden

your eldest child

bleating at your leg like a calf who doesn't see his mother

Yet I would surprise you

startle you with my manhood

not pressed against your thigh

but thrown over my shoulders

a cloak trimly fit

I would be a man
finally come upon you
all at once
a stalwart coat of arms
a rampart to shield you from the wiles of Satan

I would surprise you this year
the 12th
the holy integer of completion
I would be a man
that husband who battles beside you
that partner who com-
pletes.

My hand dives under covers
and finds its mark
straight as an arrow
and you my target

Let this be the pledge.

SALVATION, A SANDWICH

Let me speak of the love of God

         as it sits plainly in front of me

         like an open-faced peanut butter

         and jelly sandwich, amazing

         grace on one side, stern rebuke

         on the other. I take slices of bread

         into my palm, bring them together

         inches from my nose, the peanut

         butter bonding with jelly, and taste.

                  It is good.

But sometimes the two slices look like

         bricks and I decide that PB&J

         is not enough. I return to the fridge

         to find something with tomatoes

         in it. When this happens, the Lord

         will tell you, I will pay. Acid will

         climb the ladder of my throat

         until I'm sick with bile as I lie

         in bed and I will think of the verse

         in Proverbs, of dogs giving their barf

               a second look.

But on good days like this one, I'll put

the sandwich together like a toddler

learning how to feed himself. My mouth

will draw open like gates and I have

to ask: This is so delicious. How come

I get it?

Psalms 91: A Hood Translation

"You will not fear the terror of night, nor the arrow that flies by day, nor the pestilence that stalks in the darkness, nor the plague that destroys at midday. A thousand may fall at your side, ten thousand at your right hand, but it will not come near you." Verses 5-7

Listen. I have something to tell you
something to free you from the turn
of the lid on your prescription
the fermented breath of a bottle's lips
the easy flick of a lighter, the only light
you've seen in days:

Relax, I say. Things will be well.
All will turn out. That problem
you've been returning to the last
eleven nights that forces you to count
holes in the walls next to your bed
will be resolved
will fade like memory
like the scar on your abdomen
the wound you thought would never heal.

The men you owe money to will never collect.
They will either forget your debt
or accept what you give them,

but they will not take full payment
even if many years from now
you were to force cash into their palms
having so much extra to do with
as you wish.

And quit looking in the mirror.
Stop picking at that pockmark
on your cheek wondering
whether it's cancer
or kidney failure or if that body
you spent the night with
was infected.
Surely, you'll be alive many years
from today.

Don't bother to read the news;
turn off your TV.
When someone speaks of terror
of women violated in their homes
their husbands forced to watch
don't listen. Whisper,
This coat I'm wearing is bulletproof
and my blood is stubborn
my heart dutiful.

When you drive through streets
dressed in graffiti, filled with
tiny barefooted children
who stop their ghetto games
to watch you pass
their mothers watching from balconies
of unpainted apartments
and their "uncles"
standing on sidewalks with 4 or 5
angry looking young men
with faces like the barrels of
shotguns, don't trip.
They are God's children and
you will find favor in their eyes.
So wave to the gangsters.
Make small talk with the junkies.
Pat the snot faced child on the
first row of cornrows
and bow to his mother as if she were
a debutante. Be comforted.

You are saved.

LIKE CHILDREN

We live in a world where only the homeless

Seem holy.

Those who are esteemed

By Society

Bicker and slap fight

Like children.

Everywhere there are fences and locks

And the sour judgment

Of a cop. But your word,

Lord, is a rock.

Let this world be the window.

WATERFALL

I am from Fresno,
a city that is tattooed
over the width of my heart,
a city that is little more
than a tomb of poor children.

Where women leave infants
      in parked cars and scurry
            to dark apartments and hurry
                  back, fix in hand.

Where men stare angrily
      from front yards, guns
            tucked at their waists, beer
                  bottles in hand.

Where homeless veterans
      stand on countless corners
            cooing to themselves incoherently
                  sign in hand.

I grew up on these streets,

a gun tucked at my waist,

scurrying to get my fix,

a scowl for a face,

yet looking for a sign.

I thought I'd know no

other place.

But I was accepted to UC Davis,

a college three hours north.

When I graduated with a BA, I didn't

know what to do. How many

of us feel that way? Anxious.

Alone. Decisions weighing

on our shoulders like the

weight of great boulders.

My older brother, a man

I respect for his wisdom,

for his eyes with which he sees

the world a little more clearly

than the rest, for his talent

as a writer, something I'd

always wanted to be, told me,

"Don't go back to Fresno,"

pointing to the tattoo

scrawled across my forearm.
"You can't go back."

But I'd left my two children
behind, whose names I speak now
like prayers, sacred reverie:
Cruz and Marina.

I'd left their mother, a short,
dark woman
with a smile that could ignite bullets
who worked
at Walmart, that tomb of the American Dream,
to pay bills.

I was conflicted. Later that night,
after my brother's worldly wisdom
had unfurled into my ears and strangled
my heart, I dreamed:

I was at the edge of a great cliff,
rushing waters pouring over the fold
of rock, a furious waterfall.
Standing on the embankment,
I saw a tremendous ape on the other side,

waving its hands and stomping

its feet as movie apes are prone

to do. Next to me was my brother.

"Don't go near it. It will hurt you.

It may kill you," he warned. But I couldn't help

think that this wasn't your average

blood thirsty ape. Its eyes

held the tears of a small child.

Finally, the ape lost control

and tumbled over the edge. I ran across the water,

treading on it like some counterfeit prophet.

When I looked down, it was indeed the body

of my own son. Cruz. His brains shimmering

behind his head, coating the rocks below.

The next day I returned to Fresno.

I had to protect my family.

I've been trying to protect them ever since.

God gives us dreams that seem

like B movies, like the residue

of stupid youtube videos we've watched,

like fodder for bad poetry. Yet we must see.

See past the tombs, see past the faces of the lost,

see past our greatest fears. See the signs.

Cross the waterfall and embrace.

III.   THE CHOLO AND OTHER VOICES

CAMINANTE ALREDEDOR

—after Neruda's "Walking Around"

There is only light and

its absence.

There is only sight and there is

not.

Tethered to this blind meat

I walk dully down the hallways

of days

of hours

of minutes

tick tick tick

that trick

a poor sick man like me.

I hear the seconds

scratching behind thin walls.

Although I've lived here

felt moisture and particle

escape from breaks

in the shell

and although I've tried to swallow

them back

to stopper the leaks
there is no mending
what is fleeting.

And it's time
thumping thumping thumping
in my ears
damaging drywall
hammering timber
knocking picture
frames askew.

You see
the boards of this place are warped
held together by weary nails
that were always meant to fail.

At the edge of each door
I make my commotion
fingers set against jamb
I fumble in haze
thumbs writhing dumbly
my weak eyes
crescented into dim moons.
The knob is broken

or it is missing

or it is the wrong one.

I can never be sure

so I press on

sojourner of disorder

slack-footed

faint and lost in seconds

gloating between the teeth

of spent heartbeats.

I wish I had words

that could lead beyond this

oafishness of breaths

of flesh

of pores

grown wide

splitting from inside.

But I am only a worm

a root and a tomb

I do not see what makes me

stumble.

There is only light and

its absence.

There is only sight and there is

not.

Song Of The Bodybuilder

Push. Pull.

Pull. Push.

Push. Push.

Each day I begin

and begin

and begin

and begin again

if tendon holds.

I am sculpting

digging

uncovering

what is there

somewhere.

Sometimes I see it.

Myself.

My True-Self

And it shines like polished metal.

Each day I stack

and unstack.

Push. Pull.
Pull. Push.
The unpushing
becomes the pushing.

Each day is a checked box:
lats
delts
tris
pecs
I must make it new.
The burning
so it won't burn.
The increasing
so I decrease.

I wish a woman would see me.
Me of my dreams.
She could hold me in her palm
see my size
my true size.
Bulge of veins.
Flutter of heart.
Shock of salt.

O that she would spread me out

like a patient on a table

and check each box:

lats

delts

tris

pecs

She would see

I'm not like the others.

I'm bigger

so much bigger than

she imagined.

So much bigger than the

Others.

But because no one ever looks

not like I do

until then

I stand in a sea of clanks

a small man stranded

iron sounding against iron.

It's so easy to get lost.

Song Of The Ghetto Bird

"Sheriff Steve Magarian unveiled two gleaming green and gold McDonnell Douglas 500E 420-horsepower turbine-powered helicopters Wednesday to boost the Fresno County Sheriff's Department's arsenal against crime."—Fresno Bee

I am the ghetto bird,
the eye in the sky; I
whir and wind, looking
for bones and small men
who hold sabers and chop
flesh into pitiful chunks.

I see everything from here,
the streets illuminated
like filaments, like bright
stars that have imploded
into black holes. They never
sleep, these streets,
they pulsate like alveoli
stringing through the chest
of the city, this tomb of children.

I shine down ant holes,
into pathetic living
rooms with large, flickering

screens, into lost lives,

where wives cluck at men

as they recline on dingy

sofas. I see the sins of the father

stamped into the chromosomes

of the son, their skin itching,

etched with ink, as they release

smoke from their vulgar

mouths, their beards and hands

and souls smelling of beer

and motor oil, as they stare

at guns on coffee tables,

their stunted minds all the time

contemplating violence.

Their sadness plays out

before me. Nothing is hidden,

a never-ending matinee, a movie

on the big screen you would never

pay to see, the characters out-

lined in chalk.

I am proof that there is no god

above

Or Hell

below,

but only a man's conscience,

which amounts to

                                        nothing.

If I look closely enough,

if I shine down your throat,

into your heart, I can see the crimes

you'll plan before you plan

them. And that should be

                                        safety enough.

SONG OF THE GANGBANGER

You don't know what
it's like, stepping from your porch
and looking down the block,
spying fools who want to come up.
You must stay strapped. No joke.

Let's say I was to say peace,
call this nigga my brother, and put
the thang down. He'll take it
for weakness, and when you're a man,
when God put you in charge
of your woman and girl and little man,
you can't let them take you for a punk.

So I stay lit, ready for anything,
my gat loaded, my eyes loaded
red from all them trees, from all them WASPS
whispering lies about me.
I wish you could see.

SONG OF THE FALLEN ANGEL

Darkness is no place for a seraph.

Look at Me. Look at My chains,
links of ice, bound to blocks of black
fire, which singe this noble flesh.
There's no room to spread My wings,
a threescore cubit span, regal and mighty
as the day the Holy One fashioned them.

Once I was clothed in beauty, the stars
forging a brilliant crown, a nebula
for a breastplate, lightning a royal sword,
and a galaxy for My codpiece. When I spoke,
it was like thunder, like a great rush
of earthly waters, terrifying to Man.

Man, that insolent pest, that wayward beast!

Why should the Holy One view
them with such favor, these mud
infested fetuses? They betray
their father and spit at their own mother.

They are not worthy of divine love,
not like We are. But they will pay.

SONG OF THE MURDER SUICIDE

Three children. I had three children,
each with their mother's muted eyes,
her thin nose that was the length of three
of my kisses, her hands caressing
the small of my back on those nights
she looked at me, light splitting her
irises. But I don't see the light anymore.
Three months ago, she took it with her,
packed it into two of our rolling luggages,
the lone luggage left standing idly
in the garage, ignoble, burglarized of its
mates.

She's the one to steal them and she stole them too,
the three. Division by subtraction. Now five is
one.

Separation, such a lonely word:
the action or state of moving or being moved;
the division of something into constituent or distinct
elements. This and more. Dark nights without
the wafting air of conditioned hair, no children's

cough resounding under comforters,

even the family dog pouted in the corner,

the shine behind its bluish eyes hushed

into haze. I was not whole. The rest of me

had disappeared and I was left, a piece

with no peace.

And then I found them one night at her mother's

house at the bottom of a bottle of bourbon,

my salty tears serving as chaser, the sum of their parts

the portion I lacked to add everything back.

When I saw her, I leapt for her neck, tightened my rough

hands against her gentle throat, my fingers forming

an unbroken circle, two becoming one flesh, until her body

fell to the carpet, her soul escaping like a battered

housewife.

And then only the children were left. I charged, knocking

over our picture from Easter, the glass shattering

into razors, tiny effigies of brokenness, of five

who had become   one   only to become undone, cleaved into

fragments.

I held the blade above my head, summoning the courage

of everything I'd worked for, of everything I'd believed in, of everything I'd wanted, and I struck to protect the sanctity of this unity. I took their lives and then my own, piercing this family into completion.

SONG OF THE TWEAKER

I.

I won't walk without
protection, without
a gun holstered to my
hip as I mount Blackstone,
feeling the chrome shine
as if it were a luminous
Cross and I its crusader.

II.

Liquor makes the pain go
away, but meth, bright
in its bubble, gives me
the strength to tell the world
not to fuck with me.

III.

If the world is a crystal,
each person a mineral,
my stare melts each one
in the bulb, an abortion,
the lighter in my hand

triggered, the flame set
to take everyone to the Pit.

IV.

Shadows look threatening
as does everything. I picture
my children's mouths curled
in agony, the darkness
swallowing them whole,
gritting its teeth, laughter
escaping like smoke. Only
the light that reflects
off these bullets protects me.

V.

Sometimes I peer through
blinded windows and see
eyes, red and wide, glassed
over with malice, with lies.
It's the world that stares back.
And though I know there's no gun
large enough to take it all
down, I plot my revenge.

VI.

I anoint my hands
with ephedrine, slip
the clip in, cock it back.
Feel lead slide into chamber.
I take aim and won't
hesitate to squeeze, until
the world is broken, a gunshot wound blossoming,
blood assaulting asphalt,
red red roses of the streets.
See the muzzle flash, hear
the screams, and taste
what is Holy.

DANTE'S SONG

This is the pit. The crown
of Hell grows before me, jagged
spikes of its outline birthed above
the belly of a mountain.

City of Woe!

I mount brooding streets, expecting
to see bones protruding from cross-
walks, stops signs curlicued by blood,
the necks of heretics splayed across train
tracks, emaciated faces in center divides.
But they're not here.

City of Woe!

I wish to see rivers running red
from the womb of the earth,
sinners pared in the city square,
but they're not there.
Why must the truth be so harsh?
Where are the hot pokers

for singeing orifices, the three-faced
beasts chewing flesh?
No children in agony, no aborted
pedophiles with wounds steeped
in brine, no devils to speak of, only time.

City of Woe!

There is no thing in this Hell save
one thing: A single chair before a television
as wide as the scope
of your eyes, which plays
images of your life, your best
moments, your most intimate touches,
the birth of your child perhaps, her wail
as she spills forth, remnants of placenta
coating her arms.

This sounds like a good thing,
but the pain hangs dumbly
in the gullet as you view these images,
seeding despair, until you wish
they never happened, the ultimate cruelty.

EFFIGY #1: REFLECTIONS IN DUST

The mud

    Of the Grave

        Clings to Henry's boot

As he peruses the wares

    Of the vendors

        At the Cherry Auction

        A swap meet

        Filled with chicken farmers and happy daughters

Outside the

    Gangsters

        Wait

            Polishing the gun

        That will expel the bullet

And end Henry's life.

Effigy #2: Reflections In Dust

A man stands above a woman

    naked to the waist

He is giving her everything

    she could ever want

             and more

    in fact

    she says

        take it back

EFFIGY #3: REFLECTIONS IN DUST

                                               This is a

Poem for the

Dead Woman

                    Torn and Raped

          Garbage

                        and Pain

    and

               Terror

               In the Corner a Boy Weeps with what is Left

                             Broken Glass

        Arrhythmias

                                   the Smell

                    of her Perfume

    But the dead don't come back to

        Life.

JAIL CEREMONY

Whenever I get out, my girlfriend performs a ceremony.
She meets me on the street outside the jail's doors,
smoking a cigarette coolly as if she's just a nameless beauty
who walks the streets of downtown. When she sees me,
she'll act like she doesn't know me but wants to. She'll suck
on the smoke one last time, eyeing me as if I'm famous,
like one of them rappers after the show. She knows how much
I love it when she wears sandals, so she'll be wearing
new ones. She'll let the butt fall and it'll writhe there, the last
of its fire petering out, and with one firm step she'll crush
it, drive it into the concrete like a bully on a playground.

This will make me think of the power she holds over me. I'll think
of the times I'm made to rage in the innocent line of a grocery
store, her bare feet catching my eye, me losing my cool at the sight
of her perfect arches, her toes lifting up like tiny dolphins
synchronized swimming. And I know the red rose tattooed around
her right ankle is the exact width of the clasp of my hand,
thumb to forefinger. And I'll feel myself start to grow, my breath
stabbing at my chest like it does at the end of a CO's baton.

I'd like to say this is when the ceremony starts, but it starts weeks before when I know I'll be getting out, when even the shape

of my cellmate looks feminine. As I stand with everything I own

in an envelope, my girl will ask in a tough voice if I need a ride

and if she's wearing them, she'll pull her sunglasses down the length

of her nose and hold them there, her index finger pointed as if ordering

a Dog to sit. Then the feeling that begins in the blood circulating

in the meat of my thighs will rise, rest on each nerve, giving spasms

to each muscle, long pumped from push-ups, a ritual without mate.

She'll lead me by the hand to the curb where's she parked. On the long

drive home, all I can do is sit there and stare and thank God for giving

me such a woman, a woman who smells like a woman ought to smell.

When we get back to her apartment, she'll push me into the bedroom

and order me to the mattress on the floor and I'll give it all to her,

working hard as if I'm getting paid, sweat dripping from my forehead

into her mouth, her tongue catching it as if she's dying of thirst.

When we're done, we lay like that for an hour or more, not bothering

to clean up. And I'll start to think it was almost worth it, all those nights

without her, all those nights hearing rumors of fights, making meals

from the noodles of dried soups, they almost seem worth it in

> light of this ceremony.

HOMEMADE PORN

After Sharon Olds' "Sex Without Love"

"Approximately 88 percent of homemade sexual material uploaded online ends up on porn websites, a study by the Internet Watch Foundation has found."—US News

Why do they do it, these rigid, jaundiced

figures banging staccato against the floor,

the digital eye recording it for a preponderance?

It's a delicate, private piece of silver,

Love, far too meaningful to put on display,

lips splayed, hips wide, generous orifices

generously oiled until come what may.

It's a crime to debase the Holy, the accomplices

two lusty, innocent souls pounding

flesh like drums because they can, because

their tits and ass and cock are still young.

Why do they do it? I ask myself and pause:

Because it's their money shot, an exhibitionist's chance

at eternity before they exit this life and advance.

For Don Arturo, El Rey De Chicano Studies, Fresno City College

Picture it: Chicano Studies 11, 1995.
It was summer, a morning class,
on the second floor in the college's ancient
library. I remember it because the sun
was just getting riled up and the way the light
shone through the windows and reflected off
the curve of your bald head blinded me.

When you walked into the classroom
on the first day, carrying a briefcase, looking as if you were late
even though you were ten minutes early, truthfully,
I didn't think much of you. *What can this fool teach me?*
I thought to myself, my tattoos poking out of my tank top,
reading like a list of crimes committed.

Back then I'd come to the conclusion that doing dirt
for the homies was something like standing true
and strong during *Huelga* and that fighting in the streets
was the same as fighting for *El Movimiento.*

I thought I knew it all, but you helped me

to realize I knew nothing.

One day, you brought a poster
with two black children,
children so dark they could've been
Michael Jordan's own.
Across the front it stated bluntly, like a slap across
my 19 year old face, *The Legacy of Africa in Mexico.*
You told the class that slaves from Africa
brought their culture and bloodline to Mexico.
Immediately, I rejected your words, thinking
of the black Crips and black Bloods who patrolled
Fresno streets like night watchmen.

But later that night, I sat in the dark of my living room,
the *cucarachas* surrounding me like cops,
and I started to think: The only beefs I had
on the streets weren't from *negros,*
they were from other *vatos,* dudes who looked just like me.
And maybe, just maybe, the reason was because Chicanos
had been deprived of their identity and with a little
education, with a little oral tradition, with
a little Chicano Studies, a little Art Amaro,
Raza could work it out, repatriate the Southwest
and do something real for their families. I liked this idea.

I still do.

Now, when standing in front of my own CLS class,
the sunlight bouncing off my own bald head, blinding
my own bad ass students, I think of you.

Don Arturo,
the Lord only knows how much
respect and admiration
I have for you, but maybe the best way
I can show you is to tell you,
the next *pisto's* on me.

CHROME

In this dream,

I'm cleaning the barrel of a large caliber, chrome handgun in the living

room of a home I must own. The house is decorated in dark colors,

has dark oak furniture, and looks exactly the way, if I close my eyes

and think about it, I would want my house to look if I could buy one.

I'm sitting in the living room, definitely my living room, cleaning out

the barrel of this *beautiful* gun, probably a 9mm or more. It's tucked

between my legs and pointing upwards and I'm shoving the end

of this long, metal rod into the barrel over and over. Every time I pull

the rod out, black soot falls all over my newly creased khakis.

This shit's getting all over me.

I'm sitting there cleaning the gun,

and I see myself in the reflection of a huge TV that's directly across

from me. The TV's huge, 80 inches or more, but it's not on. The screen

is black and I can see my reflection perfectly like a mirror. When I notice

my reflection, I clean the barrel harder and harder.

That's when it happens.

The gun goes off.

An orange flame blazes out of the nozzle and a piece of my face falls on

my lap. I don't take my eyes off the TV screen, but I get up. The chunk of flesh slaps onto the floor. It sounds like mud. I walk out of the living room into the kitchen still holding the gun. I enter my hallway and I know it's my hallway because there's the pictures I took with my lady and the kids hanging on the wall. I enter the bathroom. It's white and clean. I look at myself in the mirror.

The gun blew off a chunk of my jawbone.
I mean there's a huge chunk of my flesh bit out of my face. Without thinking, I poke at the crater with the barrel. There's no blood, no blood at all. There's only flesh, raw and pink. I poke at the wound and get this: I'm worried about getting the gun dirty. I mean it's beautiful. It's shimmering. It's gorgeous and I don't want to get it dirty.
That's when I notice it.

There's something silver in my head.
I can barely see it through the place where I'm missing face, but it's there and it shines like a new day. I want to see more, so I raise the gun and point it at my left eyeball. I squeeze the trigger and another huge chunk of my flesh, a meaty slab as thick as tri-tip, is torn off by the bullet. I hear the gushy plop it makes on the floor. It sounds like beef being schlepped onto a grill. And it's funny, even though I blew my own eye out and it's lying on the linoleum, I can see better without it.
It's like my eyeball was holding me back.

And I can see the silver object in my head better.

It's like a metal bone and I want to see more, so I blow out my other eyeball. My eye hits the floor and somehow I can see it. It's like my vision is free. I can see behind me, below me, around me, I mean my vision is perfect and wide like a panoramic picture. I unload on the rest of my body, feeling better after every bullet carries a piece of me away until there's not even an arm left to hold that beautiful gun. I'm a 5 foot 8 inch tall, chrome cylinder. I look like a missile, smooth and shiny, so shiny, I'm almost blinding.

But then my vision starts to flicker.
I see images of myself in my living room cleaning the gun again.
I see my reflection in the TV and then it disappears and I'm back
to being a silver missile in the bathroom and then I'm back in the living
room, cleaning the gun.
Over and over.

But the last time it happens,
the last time I see my image in the living room, something is different.
I'm different. My image is completely black. No detail. No features at all.
I'm a shadow and it scares me. I'm the black image in the TV, but I want
desperately to be the silver missile. I want to shoot myself again, feel the
flesh peel off me like a layer of wet clothing.
My God, that feeling.

It felt so good,

as if, after years and years of being captive, I was

free, finally

free.

PETER RAISES THE DEAD (ACTS 9.32-42)

When the call came from Joppa, I was tempted
to ignore it. I'd had success in Lydda, having healed
Aeneas, and I found myself a local celebrity,
which wasn't too bad for an unemployed fisherman.
But You must know that. And You must know
how Your saints came marching down my block,
a wretched flock, how they tore their clothes
as they walked before they finally stopped at my door
crying, bleating. As if I were their shepherd.

It got worse: my hands grew moist as they spoke
of Tabitha, of the sudden typhoid that set her beefy
cheeks aflame, and of the still way she lay
in an upstairs room, her body rigid like the wick
of an unlit candle. How could I deny them?

You must've watched as we tread the road
to Joppa an hour later, you must've seen me swallow
hard, remembering I was a sham. I'd imagined
myself the Son of Man and made a show each time
I stepped onto the streets, pretending not to notice
the donkey dung smearing the laces of my sandals.

I'd say what I thought You'd say, pray the words
You'd pray to those who bade, stealing Your material.

Oh God, when we arrived in Joppa, Tabitha
was dead. The women on the roof of her house
gaped as I approached, their eyes grey shrouds of faith.
They took me to her body, cold as a tomb, silent
as the grave, and I ordered everyone to leave
and I puked. *Peter*, I wept, the taste of bread and wine
burning my throat, *what have you gotten yourself into?*

I thought back to Your stint on earth, to the signs
and wonders I'd watched You work, but most of the time
when You performed signs, I just wondered. It was then
I began to pray, not for the dead, but for me, Peter,
the living, the supposed rock of your church.

My prayers must've pushed a button. *Simon Peter*,
a voice called out. I raised my face from my hands,
and there was Tabitha sitting up, straight as a cross,
alive as a tree. *Get me off this table*, she said.
I wiped the tears from my eyes as I helped her down,
all the time thinking, *You saved my sorry ass once again.*

BIOLOGY 101

Go to the cell, my brother,

consider its wonders,

follow the strands down rivers

of life to the nucleus, the brain

of this fine structure, the perfect

fingerprint of the Lord.

                            Temporary

in its nature, the cell begins to die,

its rule imprinted in cytoplasm,

a microcosm of this miracle we live

in called the World. Yet this is the Word:

matter cannot be destroyed nor

forsaken and, knowing this,

carry on in eternity towards Wisdom.

TATTOOED

When I sat in His chair,
I asked the Lord to in inscribe
an image over my heart
of everything that's ever
been Holy to me, my loves,
my family, my glowing dreams,
all those things that I would kill
and be killed for, those things
that make this dark world radiate.

He sunk his needle into my
flesh, so deep that I fell asleep
and didn't wake for 40
days. When he was done,
I regained consciousness
and arose. I looked in the mirror,
the hand of God rubbing salve
into my skin, feeling like a cool
breeze, and it was beautiful.
The ink's image pulsated, light
beaconing into small, pointed
blades, little daggers of Truth.

THE CHOLO WHO SAID NOTHING

I spray paint on walls—

    all asterisks and ellipses

    the dot dot dot of a message

    you can find in Indian ink over the length of my arms

Maybe it's an image of

    hands clasped together in prayer

    with nothing between them

    praying prayers that amount to nothing

or maybe it's a bible verse

    a quote from the Book of the Irrelevant

    chapter zero

        verse nada

I am the Cholo who says nothing

You may have seen me on stage

    on screen.

You may even be sick of me

    saying to yourself

    Enough

    This is not who we are

    This is not how I want us to be represented

    The Chicano is done with the cholo!

that gangbanger hungry

for dope and his own mother's blood.

You may point

to the doctor

to the lawyer

to the dean of your college

or even the migrant farmworker

You may even hold your breath whenever you see me

on the street

on the screen

but nevertheless

generations later

Here I Am

I am the Cholo Who Will Never Say Nothing

Do Nothing

Bring Nothing to the Table

but nevertheless

Here I Am

A Big Chief in the Brown Tribe filled with Brown Pride

waiting

for someone educated

like You

to Listen

Kenneth Chacón is a native of Fresno, California where he spent much of his youth and part of his adult life involved in gangs and drugs. By the grace of God, he was able to get educated. He received his MFA from Fresno State in 2004. His work has appeared in *San Joaquin Review*, *Cimmaron Review*, *Poetry Quarterly*, *BorderSenses* among others. He lives with his wife, four children, and grandchild and teaches English and Chicano Studies at Fresno City College. He hopes that through his writing, he can reach the ones who need comfort, the hurt, the lost, the broken, and somehow, impossible as it once seemed, he can welcome light into a dark world.

Made in the USA
Las Vegas, NV
13 December 2022

62213971R00080